Contents

Introduction

The criminal justice system in Britain, operating through the police, courts, prosecution, probation and prison services, aims to:

—prevent and reduce crime where possible;

—provide effective support for the victims of crime;

—deal fairly, justly and without delay with those suspected, accused or convicted of offences;

—convict the guilty and acquit the innocent; and

—punish suitably those found guilty.

Although Britain is a unitary state, there are three systems of criminal justice—one in England and Wales, one in Scotland and the other in Northern Ireland. There are a number of differences in both law and practice in Scotland and, to a lesser extent, Northern Ireland, although the general policy objectives are the same as those for England and Wales. For example, Scotland has a different court and prosecution system and, like Northern Ireland, has separate prison and police services. These and other significant variations are described in this book.

The criminal law is interpreted by the courts, but changes in the law are normally matters for Parliament as the supreme legislative authority. Most legislation affecting criminal law is government-sponsored, usually in consultation with interested parties such as the police, the legal profession, the probation service and voluntary bodies.

In March 1991 the Government set up a Royal Commission to review the effectiveness of criminal justice in England and Wales (see p. 75). The Commission hopes to complete its work within two years.

Public expenditure on the criminal justice system in Britain has increased in real terms by 50 per cent since 1979, and in 1990–91 it stood at £11,120 million. More than two-thirds of expenditure is initially incurred by local government authorities, with the help of central government grants, mainly on the police.

Crime

Statistics

There has been a substantial increase in recorded crime since the 1950s, although an international crime survey carried out in 14 countries in 1989 showed that England and Wales, Scotland and Northern Ireland were below the average in the incidence of all crime in Western Europe, North America and Australia.

Crime tends to be concentrated in inner cities and deprived areas. The risk of burglary, for example, in inner-city areas is about twice as high as the national average. Rising affluence has provided more opportunities for casual property crime. In 1957, for example, motor-car crime was only one-tenth of total crime but this has risen to about one-third.

Most crime is committed by young males, is opportunist and is not planned by hardened professional criminals, although these do exist. Only a small proportion of young male offenders go on to become serious repeat offenders.

Measurement of Crime

The two main measures of crime in Britain are the official criminal statistics collected annually on the basis of offences recorded by the police and the figures derived from the British Crime Survey.

Notifiable Offences Recorded by the Police in England and Wales in 1990[1]

Offence Group	Recorded crimes	Crimes cleared up
Violence against the person	184,665	141,694
Sexual offences	29,044	22,041
Burglary	1,006,813	255,887
Robbery	36,195	9,574
Theft and handling stolen goods	2,374,409	709,848
Fraud and forgery	147,909	89,831
Criminal damage	553,466	120,527
Other	31,131	30,021
Total	**4,363,632**	**1,379,423**

Source: Home Office.

[1]Excludes criminal damage of £20 and under.

The Scottish police recorded 536,000 crimes in 1990, of which 32 per cent were cleared up. In Northern Ireland just over 57,000 crimes were recorded, of which 38 per cent were cleared up.

The British Crime Survey (BCS), which is a sample survey, provides estimates of the extent of various crimes, including those not reported to the police. The BCS covers violence against the person, and theft of, and damage to, private property. Respondents describe the offences they have experienced in the preceding year, so the results of the three surveys carried out in 1982, 1984 and 1988 cover crime in 1981, 1983 and 1987. A fourth survey is being conducted in England and Wales in 1992 and a separate study in Scotland in 1993.

Levels of recorded and unrecorded crime, 1987: *British Crime Survey* estimates

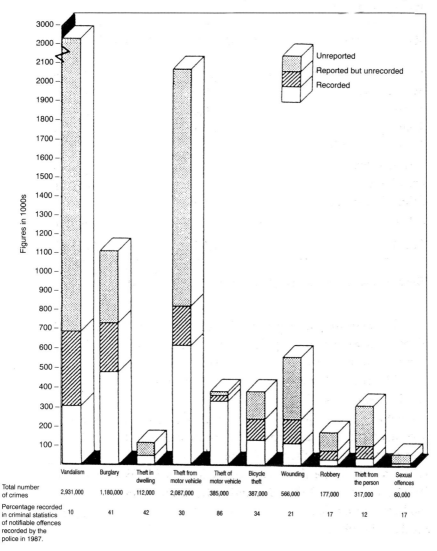

	Vandalism	Burglary	Theft in dwelling	Theft from motor vehicle	Theft of motor vehicle	Bicycle theft	Wounding	Robbery	Theft from the person	Sexual offences
Total number of crimes	2,931,000	1,180,000	112,000	2,087,000	385,000	387,000	566,000	177,000	317,000	60,000
Percentage recorded in criminal statistics of notifiable offences recorded by the police in 1987.	10	41	42	30	86	34	21	17	12	17

Source: *The 1988 British Crime Survey.* Home Office Research Study 111.

The 1988 BCS estimates (see graph on p. 5) were derived by applying rates from the 'core' sample of respondents (11,741 people, including an ethnic minority sample of 1,349 Afro-Caribbeans and Asians) to the household and adult populations in England and Wales. Confirming a number of results from the two earlier surveys, the 1988 estimates illustrated the predominance of offences against property in the BCS crime count (particularly those relating to motor vehicles), the shortfall between survey estimates of offences committed and the number recorded by the police, and the extent to which different types of offences are reported to the police.

Prevention

The Government believes that successful crime prevention, which it regards as the best way of dealing with crime, requires a partnership between central and local government, relevant public services and agencies, industry and commerce, voluntary organisations, schools, parents and committed individuals.

Government Bodies

The national crime prevention programme is overseen by the Ministerial Group on Crime Prevention, consisting of ministers and officials from 13 government departments. It considers appropriate responses to emerging problems and the results of recent research, and also seeks to keep crime prevention on the agenda for action by each government department.

The Ministerial Group's secretariat is provided by the Home Office Crime Prevention Unit, which was set up in 1983. In Scotland, a Scottish Office Group on Crime Prevention disseminates the policies of the Group, while in Northern Ireland an

Inter-Departmental Group on Crime Prevention co-ordinates a response to crime. Research support for the Ministerial Group is supplied by the Home Office, whose research programmes have led to the development of the inter-agency approach as a method of preventing crime at the local level.

The Home Office Standing Conference on Crime Prevention was established in 1985 to bring together representatives of central and local government, the police, industry, commerce and voluntary bodies. Working groups look in detail at specific issues and the consequent reports are considered by the Home Office.

The Police

Each of the 52 police forces in Britain (see p. 15) is responsible for crime prevention in its area, taking into account the views and opinions of consultative groups and eliciting their co-operation.

The police service employs some 800 crime prevention officers, who work mainly out of uniform and provide specialist advice to people wishing to safeguard their property. Many police forces also have architectural liaison officers who analyse planning applications for large building projects and make recommendations for reducing opportunities for criminals.

Government Campaigns and Information

The Government has for many years financed information and publicity campaigns designed to encourage crime prevention by the public.

For example, 'Crime Prevention Week', which took place during April 1991, was the largest event of its kind ever conducted in Britain. The campaign involved advertising on television and radio, in the national and local press, and on over 3,000 billboard poster sites throughout England and Wales. Thousands of people were involved in hundreds of local and national events publicising ways to beat crime, a different aspect of which was highlighted on each day of the week. A number of prominent companies also supported Crime Prevention Week with promotions, special offers and competitions. An equally extensive campaign—Car Crime Prevention Year—is taking place throughout 1992.

Crime Prevention News is a quarterly publication produced by the Home Office and circulated to crime prevention activists and interested groups and individuals. Scotland has its own quarterly crime prevention newsletter entitled *Crime Cracker*.

Inner-City Initiatives

Under the Government's Safer Cities Programme, launched in 1988, crime prevention projects are underway in 20 inner-city areas across England. The object of the projects is to tackle identified crime problems through well-targeted crime prevention activity. Each project is led by a local committee drawn from local agencies and supported by a co-ordinator financed by the Home Office.

The Scottish Safer Cities programme presently comprises two projects in Glasgow and one each in Edinburgh and Dundee. A fifth project is being established in Aberdeen.

Crime prevention measures form an important element in programmes established by the Department of the Environment, such as Estate Action and the Priority Estates Project, which aim to improve the quality of life on run-down inner-city housing estates.

The Government's inner-city Task Forces, set up to co-ordinate economic and social regeneration, support crime prevention where this is linked to the provision of employment and training opportunities for local people. Similar support is provided through the Urban Programme in Scotland.

Community Involvement

Crime Concern, the national crime prevention organisation in England and Wales, was launched in 1988 with Home Office funding. It works closely with the police, local authorities, voluntary organisations and business to stimulate and support crime prevention activity in communities. Crime Concern Scotland was established in 1989.

Neighbourhood watch schemes have grown rapidly since their inception in 1982. There are currently 92,000 schemes in England and Wales covering 5 million households. Residents of watch areas are encouraged to look out for suspicious behaviour and to report it to the police. Each scheme has a co-ordinator who acts as a contact point with the police and members of the scheme. There are some 2,000 watch schemes in Scotland.

Local crime prevention panels, of which there are over 400 in England and Wales, are designed to foster co-operation between the public and the police by undertaking and supporting crime prevention projects. Their membership is drawn from the police, local government, local businesses, voluntary and statutory agencies and the local press. There are 150 crime prevention panels in Scotland, including youth panels.

Role of Business

As well as encouraging businesses to take part directly in inter-agency crime prevention schemes, the Government aims to promote improved business practices that deter crime[1] and the incorporation of anti-crime measures into product and building design and planning.

Victim Support

The Government recognises that victims of crime should be given proper consideration and, where appropriate, compensation. There are, for instance, more than 375 victim-support schemes covering 97 per cent of the population in England and Wales, and involving over 7,000 volunteers who offer practical and emotional help. They are co-ordinated by a national organisation, Victim Support, which receives a government grant. The Government also finances the local schemes to meet either the salaries of co-ordinators or running costs. Victim Support is also established in Northern Ireland, and a similar scheme operates in Scotland.

In February 1990 the Government published its *Victim's Charter*, setting out for the first time the rights and expectations of those people who become victims of crime and the standards of service which they are entitled to expect from criminal justice agencies.

Innocent victims of violent crime in England, Wales and Scotland, including foreign nationals, may be eligible for compensation under the Criminal Injuries Compensation Scheme, whether or not the assailant is caught or convicted. The scheme also applies to people injured in the course of preventing crime or assisting the police. It is administered by a Board. Compensation is based on common-law damages and is a lump-sum

[1] A Home Office survey has shown that business crime costs over £10,000 million a year.

payment. Annual payments from the scheme have more than doubled in the last five years, from £52 million in 1986–87 to over £125 million in 1991–92.

In Northern Ireland there is separate, statutory provision in certain circumstances for compensation to be made from public funds for criminal injuries, and for malicious damage to property, including the resulting loss of profits.

In February 1990 Britain ratified the Council of Europe Convention on the Compensation of Victims of Violent Crime, under which mutual arrangements for compensation apply to citizens of those countries in which the Convention is in force.

The Government is examining how mediation and reparation schemes can help victims of crime. Experimental projects have been funded, involving the opportunity for offender and victim, if they wish, to meet and discuss the crime.

Strengthening the Law

Criminal law has evolved in response to changes in the nature of crime. A programme of legislative reform since 1984 has re-defined police powers (see p. 21), toughened penalties for drug trafficking, tackled public order issues and tightened the law on the control of firearms. The programme has also created a new structure for bringing prosecutions in England and Wales (see p. 28), applying nationally consistent standards.

Under legislation passed since 1986, the courts have powers to trace, freeze and confiscate the proceeds of drug trafficking. A court can issue an order requiring the offender to pay an amount equal to the full value of the proceeds arising from the trafficking. The laundering of money associated with illegal trafficking is unlawful. Because of the international nature of the problem, restraint and confiscation orders made by courts can be enforced against assets held overseas, and *vice versa*. These arrangements apply to countries with which mutual enforcement agreements have been concluded.

New powers adopted under legislation passed in 1990 have enabled Britain to ratify international conventions enhancing criminal justice co-operation between countries, particularly against drug dealing and fraud.

A Serious Fraud Office (see p. 30), with wide powers to investigate and prosecute serious or complex fraud in England, Wales and Northern Ireland, was established in 1988. Fraud in Scotland is investigated and prosecuted under the direction of the Lord Advocate. A court may make a confiscation order against the proceeds arising from fraud, as well as from other offences such as robbery, blackmail and insider dealing in shares.

Legislation was passed in 1988 to increase controls on firearms and, for England and Wales, the carrying of knives. The private ownership of certain highly dangerous types of weapon such as high-powered self-loading rifles and burst-fire weapons is prohibited. The police have increased powers to regulate the possession, safekeeping and movement of shotguns and firearms. Similar legislation applies in Northern Ireland. It is unlawful to manufacture, sell or import certain weapons such as knuckle-dusters or, in England and Wales, to carry a knife in a public place without good reason. The Government has proposed that responsibility for firearms licensing in England, Wales and Scotland should pass from the police to a national civilian control board.

The Public Order Act 1986, and similar legislation in Northern Ireland, strengthened the law against incitement to racial hatred and created a new offence of possessing inflammatory material. It also introduced, in England and Wales, a new order for convicted football hooligans to prevent them attending certain matches, and created a new offence of disorderly conduct to enable police to deal with hooligan behaviour. The Act additionally gave the police powers to impose conditions on assemblies in public places.

The Criminal Justice Act 1991, most of the provisions of which come into effect in October 1992, has made a number of reforms to the criminal law in England and Wales.

Measures to Combat Terrorism

Legislation provides the authorities with certain exceptional powers for dealing with and preventing terrorist activities, while taking account of the need to achieve a proper balance between the safety of the public and the rights of the individual.

Northern Ireland

The security forces in Northern Ireland have special powers to search, question and arrest. Legislation allows terrorist organisations to be proscribed by the Government. Terrorist offences which are tried on indictment are heard and dealt with in the Crown Court by a single judge sitting alone without a jury, largely because of the possibility of jurors being intimidated by terrorist organisations. The maximum period for which the police can hold a suspected terrorist on their own authority has been reduced from 72 to 48 hours, although he or she can be held for up to a further five days with the consent of the Secretary of State.

Nobody can be imprisoned for political beliefs. All prisoners, except those awaiting trial, have been found guilty in court of criminal offences. The legislation is reviewed annually by an independent person whose reports are presented to Parliament.

Other Legislation

The Prevention of Terrorism (Temporary Provisions) Act 1989, renewable annually by Parliament, provides for the exclusion from Great Britain, Northern Ireland or the United Kingdom of people connected with terrorism related to Northern Ireland affairs and for the banning of terrorist organisations in Great Britain. It also gives the police powers to arrest suspects without warrant and hold them for 48 hours and, with the approval of the Secretary of State, for up to a further five days. This provision also applies to suspected international terrorists.

It is a criminal offence to finance terrorism or receive funds for use in the furtherance of terrorism. Police can apply for a court order to freeze a suspect's assets once he or she has been charged. Funds can be confiscated if a person is convicted. The legislation allows for reciprocal enforcement agreements with other countries.

Britain attaches great importance to international action to combat terrorism and plays an active part in the work of various bodies, such as the Trevi group of European Community ministers, which facilitates police co-operation and the exchange of information about terrorism and other international crime affecting member countries. The British Government believes that there should be no concessions to terrorist demands and that international co-operation is essential in tracking down terrorists and impeding their movement from one country to another.

The Police and their Powers

Organisation

There are 43 police forces in England and Wales, eight in Scotland and one in Northern Ireland (the Royal Ulster Constabulary). Outside London the service is organised on a county basis (regional in Scotland), although some counties and regions have combined forces. The Metropolitan Police Force and the City of London force are responsible for policing London. At the end of 1990 police strength in Britain was just over 149,000, of which the Royal Ulster Constabulary numbered over 8,200.

Each force has an attachment of volunteer special constables who perform police duties in their spare time, acting mainly as auxiliaries to the regular force. They are unpaid, although the Government is considering introducing a pilot scheme to pay a bounty to special constables as part of a series of measures to boost recruitment. In Northern Ireland there is a 4,600-strong part-time and full-time paid reserve.

Police forces are maintained in England and Wales by committees of local county councillors and magistrates, and in Scotland by regional and islands councils. The Home Secretary is responsible for London's Metropolitan Police Force. In Northern Ireland the police force is responsible to a body appointed by the Government.

Chief constables are in charge of their police forces and are responsible for the appointment, promotion and discipline of all ranks below assistant chief constable. They are generally answerable to the police authorities on matters of efficiency, and must submit an annual report.

The police authorities appoint the chief constable and other top officers. They also fix the maximum permitted strength of the force, subject to approval by the appropriate Secretary of State, and provide buildings and equipment. In the Metropolitan Police area the commissioner of police and his immediate subordinates are appointed on the recommendation of the Home Secretary.

The police service is financed by central and local government. The total police budget in England and Wales in 1990–91 was about £4,500 million.

A wide-ranging review of the police service was announced by the Government in May 1992. This inquiry will report by the end of May 1993.

Central Authorities

The Home Secretary and the Secretaries of State for Scotland and Northern Ireland approve the appointment of chief, deputy and assistant chief constables. Where necessary they can:

—require a police authority to retire a chief constable in the interests of efficiency;

—call for a report from a chief constable on matters relating to local policing; or

—institute a local inquiry.

These ministers can also make regulations covering:

—qualifications for appointment, promotion and retirement;

—discipline;

—hours of duty, leave, pay and allowances; and

—uniform.

Some of these regulations are first negotiable within the Police Negotiating Board for the United Kingdom. The Board consists of an independent chairman and representatives of the police authorities, police staff associations and the home departments.

With the exception of the Metropolitan Police, all police forces are subject to statutory inspection by inspectors of constabulary reporting to central government. On request, the inspectorate also undertakes inspections of selected parts of the Metropolitan Police.

Members of the police service may not belong to a trade union nor may they withdraw their labour in furtherance of a trade dispute. All ranks, however, have their own staff associations to represent their interests.

Co-ordination of Police Operations

Several common services are provided by central government and by arrangements between forces. In England and Wales the most important of these cover forensic science, telecommunications and central and provincial criminal records. In Scotland the main common services are centralised police training, the Scottish Crime Squad and the Scottish Criminal Record Office.

Certain special services such as liaison with the International Criminal Police Organisation (Interpol) are provided for other British forces by the Metropolitan Police. The National Drugs Intelligence Unit assists police forces and the Customs service throughout Britain. A new National Criminal Intelligence Service has been set up to co-ordinate and analyse intelligence related to criminal activities. This service will bring together a number of units, including the National Drugs Intelligence Unit and the Interpol Bureau.

The services of the Fraud Squad, which is run jointly by the Metropolitan Police and City of London Police to investigate company frauds, are available in England and Wales.

Regional crime squads, co-ordinated at national level in England and Wales, deal with serious crimes such as drug trafficking and are used whenever operations cannot be dealt with by individual police forces alone.

In all areas of police work the use of scientific aids is widespread. A national police computer helps to rationalise records and speed up the dissemination of information.

Police Discipline

A British chief officer may be sued or prosecuted for any wrongful act committed by one of his or her constables carrying out duties. Police discipline codes are designed to prevent any abuse of police powers and to maintain public confidence in the impartiality of the service.

Police Complaints Authority

The independent Police Complaints Authority, established under the Police and Criminal Evidence Act 1984, has powers to:

—supervise the investigation of serious complaints against any police officer in the 43 forces of England and Wales; and

—take the final decision on whether a police officer should be charged with a breach of discipline.

If a police officer is accused of killing or seriously injuring someone, the Authority *must* supervise the investigation. If a police officer is said to have committed a serious criminal offence, the Authority is always informed immediately and then decides whether to supervise the investigation. The Authority may also supervise any investigation when it considers that it would be in the public interest to do so or if a chief officer of a force or a local police authority asks for its independent help.

If the report of an investigation indicates that a criminal offence may have been committed by a police officer, and the chief officer of the force believes that the officer should be charged, he has to send the evidence to the Crown Prosecution Service (CPS), which is completely independent of the police. If the chief officer does not do so, the Authority can insist that the case be pursued. This can result in the officer concerned being prosecuted. If the law has not been broken, the chief officer reviews the case and may recommend that the officer concerned should be charged with a disciplinary offence. If he does not do so, the Authority has the right to insist upon a charge and that the officer be brought before a disciplinary hearing.

The Authority also deals with complaints relating to the British Transport Police, the Ministry of Defence Police, Port of Liverpool Police, Port of London Authority Police and UK Atomic Energy Authority Constabulary.

Scotland and Northern Ireland
In Scotland complaints against police officers involving allegations of any form of criminal conduct are investigated by an independent procurator fiscal service. In Northern Ireland the Independent Commission for Police Complaints is required to supervise

the investigation of a complaint regarding death or serious injury and has the power to supervise that of any other complaint if it so wishes. In certain circumstances, the Secretary of State may direct the Commission to supervise the investigation of matters that are not the subject of a formal complaint.

Community Relations

Virtually all police forces have liaison departments designed to develop closer contact between the force and the community, and almost all areas have police/community consultative groups. Particular efforts are made to develop relations with young people, through greater contact with schools. School governing bodies and head teachers have a statutory obligation to describe in their annual reports the steps they take to strengthen their schools' links with the community, including the police.

Emphasis has been placed on improving relations with ethnic minorities. The Government believes that all police officers should receive a thorough training in community and race relations. The Home Office sponsors national courses in these subjects for community liaison officers and police managers, and there is also a national specialist support unit which makes a valuable contribution to improving community and race relations training for the police. Discriminatory behaviour by police officers is an offence under the Police Discipline Code. The Home Office organises recruitment advertising campaigns in the press in order to encourage black and Asian recruits to the police. In December 1990 there were 1,418 ethnic minority police officers in England and Wales.

Police Powers

Officers in Great Britain do not normally carry firearms, although in an emergency they can be issued quickly on the authority of a senior officer. Because of the terrorist campaigns in Northern Ireland, police officers there are issued with firearms for personal protection and other firearms are available for duty purposes.

Under legislation passed in 1985, the Government can authorise interception of postal and telephone services by the police in order to prevent and detect serious crime, or, in some cases, safeguard national security. The other ground for interception is the safeguarding of Britain's economic well-being. Any interception outside these procedures is a criminal offence.

Under the Police and Criminal Evidence Act 1984, a police officer in England and Wales has a general power of stop and search if he or she has reasonable grounds for suspicion that a person is carrying stolen goods, offensive weapons or implements that could be used for theft, burglary and other offences. The officer must, however, state and record the grounds for taking this action and what, if anything, was found.

Arrest

In England and Wales the police have wide powers to arrest suspects with or without a warrant issued by a magistrate. For serious offences, known as 'arrestable offences', a suspect can be arrested without a warrant. This covers all offences for which a maximum period of five years' imprisonment can be imposed on conviction. Crimes such as murder, rape and serious sexual offences against children are classified as 'serious arrestable offences'. For lesser offences, arrest without warrant exists only when certain criteria are met, for instance, if it is not possible or appropriate to send out a summons to appear in court.

Detention, Treatment and Questioning

Codes of practice issued by the Government under the 1984 Act (and since revised with effect from 1 April 1991), regulate the detention, treatment and questioning of suspects by the police in England and Wales. Failure to comply with the provisions can render a police officer liable to disciplinary proceedings. Evidence obtained in breach of the codes may be ruled inadmissible in court.

The police must open a custody record as soon as practicable for each person who is brought to a police station under arrest or is arrested at a station having attended there voluntarily. The custody officer is responsible for the accuracy and completeness of the custody record, all entries in which must be timed and signed by the maker. A person leaving police detention should be supplied on request with a copy of the record.

Following arrest, the custody officer must inform suspects of their rights. An arrested person has a statutory right to consult a solicitor—whether in private, in writing or on the telephone—and to ask the police to notify a relative or other named person likely to take an interest in his or her welfare. He or she also has the right to consult the police codes of practice. Where a person has been arrested in connection with a serious arrestable offence, but has not yet been charged, the police may delay for up to 36 hours the exercise of these rights in the interests of the investigation if certain strict criteria are met.

The police must caution a suspect before any questions are put for the purpose of obtaining evidence. The caution informs the suspect that he or she is entitled to refuse to answer questions—the so-called 'right of silence'. Questions relating to an offence may normally not be put to a person after he or she has been charged with that offence or informed that he or she may be prosecuted for it.

No police officer may try to obtain answers to questions or to elicit a statement from a person being interviewed through the use of oppression. The tape-recording of interviews with suspected offenders at police stations became standard practice from the end of 1991 and a code of practice governing these tape-recordings has been approved by Parliament.

The length of time a suspect can be held in police custody without charge is strictly regulated. For lesser offences this may not exceed 24 hours. A person suspected of committing a serious arrestable offence can be detained for up to 96 hours without charge but only beyond 36 hours if a warrant is obtained from a magistrates' court. Reviews must be made of a person's detention at regular intervals—six hours after initial detention and thereafter every nine hours as a maximum—to check whether the criteria for detention are still satisfied. If they are not, the person must be released immediately.

In any period of 24 hours a detained person must be allowed a continuous period of at least eight hours for rest, free from questioning, travel or other interruption arising out of the investigation concerned. Police cells accommodating detainees must be adequately lit, heated, cleaned and ventilated. Access to toilet and washing facilities must be provided, as well as suitable food and clothing.

A person who thinks that the grounds for detention are unlawful may apply to the High Court for a writ of habeas corpus against the person who detained him or her, requiring that person to appear before the court to justify the detention. Habeas corpus proceedings take precedence over others. Similar procedures apply in Northern Ireland, and a similar remedy is available to anyone who is unlawfully detained in Scotland.

Charging

Once there is sufficient evidence, the police have to decide whether or not to charge the person with the offence. As an alternative to charging immediately, they can, for example, decide to defer charging or to take no further action and release the person with or without bail. They may also issue a caution which is a warning that prosecution is likely for a second offence.

If charged with an offence, a person may be kept in custody if there is a risk that he or she might fail to appear in court or might interfere with the administration of justice. A young person may also be detained for his or her protection. When no such considerations apply, the person must be released on or without bail. Where someone is detained after charge, he or she must be brought before a magistrates' court quickly. This will usually be no later than the following working day.

Scotland

In Scotland the police may detain and question a suspected person for a period of up to six hours. After this period the person must either be released or charged. Once a person has been charged with a criminal offence, only voluntary statements will normally be allowed in evidence at the trial. The court will reject statements unless satisfied that they have been fairly obtained. In many areas there is tape recording of interviews with suspects in police stations. Anyone arrested must be brought before a court with the least possible delay (generally not later than the first day after being taken into custody), or—in less serious cases—liberated by the police, often on a written undertaking to attend court.

Where an accusation of a more serious offence is to be made, the accused ('defendant' is not a Scottish legal term) is brought before the sheriff for judicial examination in private. This process gives the accused an early opportunity of stating his or her position with regard to the charge. At the judicial examination, the procurator fiscal moves for committal of the accused for further examination or trial and the sheriff grants the motion unless bail is given. A maximum of eight days may elapse between committal for further examination and committal for trial. No evidence needs to be presented to the sheriff for such committal.

Awaiting Trial

There are time limits on the period a defendant may be remanded in custody awaiting trial in England and Wales. In cases tried before a magistrates' court the limits are 56 days from first appearance to trial or 70 days between first appearance to committal for trial in the Crown Court. The limit in Crown Court cases is 112 days from committal to taking of the plea. When a time limit expires, the defendant is entitled to bail unless the court extends the limit. It can only do this if satisfied that there is a good and sufficient reason and that the prosecution has acted expeditiously.

Bail

Bail is the release of an accused person in return for a sum of money payable if the accused fails to appear in court for trial. Most accused people are released on bail pending trial. They are not remanded in custody except where strictly necessary. In England and Wales, the court decides whether a defendant should be released on bail. Unconditional bail may only be withheld if the court has substantial grounds for believing that the accused would:

—abscond;

—commit an offence;

—interfere with witnesses; or

—otherwise obstruct the course of justice.

A court may also impose conditions before granting bail. If bail is refused, the defendant may apply to a High Court judge or to the Crown Court for bail. An application can also be made to the Crown Court for conditions imposed by a magistrates' court to be varied.

In some cases a court may grant bail to a defendant on condition that he or she lives in an approved bail or probation/bail hostel. Approved hostels are a valuable way of providing closely supervised accommodation for those whom the courts might otherwise remand in custody. The Government is increasing the number of places available at approved hostels, and is also aiming to encourage the development of specialist bail accommodation and supervision for those who appear to be mentally disturbed, or who have problems with alcohol or drug abuse.

The probation service has developed bail information schemes which provide the Crown Prosecution Service (CPS) with verified information about a defendant. This assists the CPS when it takes decisions on whether to oppose bail and enables the courts to take an informed decision on whether to grant bail.

The Government is taking steps to reduce the incidence of continued criminal activities by some offenders while on bail.

Scotland

Anyone accused of a crime, except murder or treason, is entitled to apply for release on bail. Even in cases of murder or treason, bail may be granted at the discretion of the Lord Advocate or a quorum of the High Court. There is a right of appeal to the High Court by the accused person against the refusal of bail, or by the prosecutor against the granting of bail, or by either party against the conditions imposed.

If a person charged with a more serious offence is kept in custody awaiting trial, the trial must begin within 110 days. The trial of a person charged with a summary offence and held in custody must begin within 40 days of the date of first appearance in court. A person in custody has the statutory right to an interview with a solicitor before he or she appears in court.

Criminal Courts

Prosecution

England and Wales

Once the police have decided to institute criminal proceedings against a person, the Crown Prosecution Service assumes control of the case, reviews the evidence and then decides whether to prosecute. The CPS, set up in 1986, is an independent government department headed by the Director of Public Prosecutions (DPP). The DPP is answerable to Parliament through the Attorney General, who is the Government's chief Law Officer.

The Service is independent of the police. It is divided into 31 areas, each of which is run by a locally-based Chief Crown Prosecutor appointed by the Director. CPS lawyers prosecute in the magistrates' courts while barristers for the Service appear in the Crown Court.

The CPS operates in accordance with the Code for Crown Prosecutors, a public document published annually in the Director's report to the Attorney General. Under the Code, a prosecution should not be started or continued unless the Prosecutor is satisfied that there is admissible, substantial and reliable evidence that a criminal offence has been committed. Once the Prosecutor is satisfied that the evidence can justify proceedings, he or she must also consider whether the public interest requires proceedings to take place. Cases in which a prosecution is considered to be inappropriate for either of these reasons are discontinued. Although the decision to prosecute is generally delegated to the lawyers in the area offices, some especially sensitive or complex cases are dealt with by the headquarters of the CPS, including terrorist offences and breaches of the Official Secrets Acts.

In 1990–91 the CPS completed proceedings relating to approximately 1.6 million defendants in the magistrates' courts and 146,000 in the Crown Court. Each CPS area is inspected regularly by a National Field Inspectorate in order to examine its effectiveness and efficiency.

Scotland

Discharging his duties through the Crown Office and Procurator Fiscal Service, the Lord Advocate is responsible for prosecutions in the High Court of Justiciary, sheriff courts and district courts. There is no general right of private prosecution. The permanent adviser to the Lord Advocate on prosecution matters is the Crown Agent, who is head of the procurator fiscal service and is assisted in the Crown Office by a staff of legally qualified civil servants.

Prosecutions in the High Court of Justiciary are prepared by procurators fiscal and Crown Office officials. They are conducted by the Lord Advocate, the Solicitor General for Scotland (the Lord Advocate's ministerial deputy) and advocates depute, who are collectively known as Crown Counsel.

Crimes tried before the sheriff and district courts are prepared and prosecuted by procurators fiscal. The police and other law enforcement agencies investigate crimes and offences and report to the procurator fiscal, who decides whether to prosecute, subject to the directions of Crown Counsel. The police cannot initiate criminal proceedings.

When dealing with minor crime, the procurator fiscal has the option of using alternatives to prosecution, such as formal warnings, diversion to social work and offers of fixed penalties. In the latter case, the offender is not obliged to accept such an offer, but if he or she does the prosecution loses the right to prosecute.

Northern Ireland

The Director of Public Prosecutions for Northern Ireland, who is responsible to the Attorney General, prosecutes all offences tried on indictment, and may do so in other (summary) cases. Most summary offences are prosecuted by the police.

Prosecutions for Fraud

The Serious Fraud Office (SFO), which started operations in 1988, investigates and prosecutes the most serious and complex cases of fraud in England, Wales and Northern Ireland. Other fraud cases are generally dealt with by the Crown Prosecution Service. The SFO is accountable through its Director to the Attorney General and to Parliament. Investigations are conducted by inter-disciplinary teams of lawyers, accountants, police officers and others with experience of investigating fraud. Most of the police officers are members of the Metropolitan Police and the City of London Police.

The SFO has powers to issue notices requiring persons to give information or produce relevant documents. Many notices are issued to banks, accountants and other similar institutions and professionals who have innocently obtained information and documents relevant to a fraud because, for example, the suspect has accounts at a particular bank. Information obtained from a potential defendant under questioning by the SFO can only be used against him or her in any subsequent proceedings if the defendant makes an inconsistent statement during the trial.

In Scotland the Crown Office Fraud Unit investigates and prepares prosecutions against fraud in co-operation with the police and other agencies, and has similar investigatory powers to those available to the SFO.

Courts

England and Wales

Criminal offences are grouped into three categories. Very serious offences such as murder, manslaughter, rape and robbery are tried only on indictment (formal accusation) in the Crown Court, where all contested trials are presided over by a judge sitting with a jury. Summary offences—the least serious offences and the majority of criminal cases—are tried only by unpaid lay magistrates or by a few paid stipendiary magistrates, sitting without a jury.

A third category of offences (such as theft, burglary or malicious wounding) are known as 'either way' offences. The magistrates decide whether to try such cases or send them to the Crown Court. If the magistrates decide to try a case summarily, they have to seek the consent of the defendant. If the defendant chooses trial by jury, the case goes to the Crown Court.

All those charged with offences to be tried in the Crown Court must first appear in front of magistrates who decide whether or not to commit them to the Crown Court for trial.

A magistrates' court, which is open to the public and the media, usually consists of three lay magistrates—known as justices of the peace—who are advised on points of law and procedure by a legally qualified clerk or a qualified assistant. There are nearly

28,000 lay magistrates. The few full-time, legally qualified stipendiary magistrates may sit alone and usually preside in courts in urban areas where the workload is heavy.

Cases involving people under 17 (soon to be 18, under the provisions of the Criminal Justice Act 1991) are heard in juvenile courts (to become youth courts in October 1992). These are specialist magistrates' courts which either sit apart from other courts or are held at a different time. Restrictions are placed on access by ordinary members of the public and media reports must not identify a young person appearing either as a defendant (unless a judge directs otherwise) or a witness.

Where a young person under 17 is charged jointly with someone of 17 or over, the case is heard in an ordinary magistrates' court or the Crown Court. If the young person is found guilty, the court may transfer the case to a juvenile court for sentence unless satisfied that it is undesirable to do so.

The Crown Court sits at about 90 centres in England and Wales and is presided over by High Court judges, full-time 'Circuit Judges'[1] and part-time Recorders. Cases received from the magistrates' courts as committals for trial form the largest element of Crown Court workload. In 1990 just over 103,000 cases were received for trial in the Crown Court, representing a four per cent increase on receipts in 1989 and almost double the level received in 1980 (55,594).

---

[1] England and Wales are divided into six circuits for the purpose of hearing criminal cases. Each circuit is divided into areas containing a centre or centres of the High Court and a Crown Court. The six circuits are: Midland and Oxford, North-Eastern, Northern, South-Eastern (including London), Wales and Chester, and Western.

In cases of serious or complex fraud, full committal proceedings in magistrates' courts may be bypassed at the discretion of the prosecution. However, there is a special procedure under which the accused can apply to the Crown Court to be discharged on the ground that there is no case to answer.

Scotland

The High Court of Justiciary is Scotland's supreme criminal court. Sitting in Edinburgh and other major Scottish towns and cities, it tries the most serious crimes and has exclusive jurisdiction in cases involving murder, treason and rape. The sheriff court is concerned with less serious offences, and the district court with minor offences.

Criminal cases in Scotland are heard either under solemn or summary procedure. In solemn procedure, the trial takes place before a judge sitting with a jury of 15 people. Details of the alleged offence are set out in a document called an indictment. The judge decides questions of law and the jury questions of fact. In summary procedure the judge sits without a jury and decides questions of fact and law.

All cases in the High Court and the more serious ones in sheriff courts are tried by a judge and jury. Summary procedure is used in the less serious cases in the sheriff courts, and in all cases in the district courts. District court judges are lay justices of the peace. In Glasgow there are also stipendiary magistrates who are full-time lawyers with the same criminal jurisdiction in summary procedure as a sheriff.

Children under 16 who have committed an offence are normally dealt with by children's hearings (see p. 67).

Northern Ireland

Summary offences are heard in magistrates' courts by a legally qualified resident magistrate. Offenders under 17 are dealt with by a juvenile court consisting of a legally qualified resident magistrate and two lay members (at least one of whom must be a woman) specially trained to deal with juveniles.

The Crown Court deals with criminal trials on indictment. It is served by High Court and county court judges. Proceedings are heard by a single judge, and all contested cases, other than those involving offences specified under emergency legislation (called 'scheduled offences'), take place before a jury.

Those persons accused of terrorist offences are tried in non-jury courts. The onus remains on the prosecution to prove guilt beyond reasonable doubt and the defendant has the right to be represented by a lawyer of his or her choice. The judge must set out in a written statement the reasons for convicting and there is an automatic right of appeal against conviction and sentence on points of fact as well as of law.

In 1990 some 43 per cent of defendants who pleaded not guilty to all charges in the non-jury courts were found not guilty.

Trial

Criminal trials in Britain have two parties—the prosecution and the defence. The law presumes the innocence of an accused person until guilt has been proved beyond reasonable doubt. An accused person has the right to employ a legal adviser and may be granted legal aid from public funds (see p. 72). If remanded in custody, he or she may be visited by a legal adviser to ensure a properly prepared defence.

Disclosure to the Defence

It is for the prosecution to prove that the defendant committed the crime alleged. In order for the defendant to understand the nature of the case against him or her, he or she must be informed of all the relevant information that the prosecution has, whether or not it forms part of its case.

In England and Wales, where cases are to be tried in the Crown Court, the Crown Prosecution Service must also disclose all the statements from the prosecution witnesses upon whom it proposes to rely. This must be done before any committal proceedings begin. This duty does not apply to offences tried in the magistrates' court, except when advance information is requested by the defence in those cases which could be tried either by magistrates or in the Crown Court.

In Scotland the prosecution must give the defence advance notice of the witnesses it intends to call and of the documents and other items on which it will rely.

Trial Procedure

Criminal trials are normally in open court and rules of evidence, which are concerned with the proof of facts, are rigorously applied. If evidence is improperly admitted, a conviction can be quashed on appeal.

During the trial the defendant has the right to hear and cross-examine witnesses for the prosecution. He or she can call his or her own witnesses who, if they will not attend voluntarily, may be legally compelled to do so. The defendant can also address the court in person or through a lawyer, the defence having the right to the last speech at the trial before the judge sums up the evidence for the jury. The defendant cannot be questioned without consenting to be sworn as a witness in his or her own defence. When he or she does testify, cross-examination about character or other conduct may be made only in exceptional circumstances. Generally the prosecution may not introduce such evidence. In Northern Ireland the judge can draw inferences from a refusal by a defendant to give evidence.

Child Witnesses

In England, Wales and Northern Ireland, child witnesses in cases involving offences of sex, violence or cruelty may now give evidence in Crown Court proceedings from outside the courtroom by means of a live television link. In this way the child need not see his or her alleged attacker in court. A child's sworn statement no longer has to be corroborated by other evidence for the court to hear it. In Scotland similar provisions apply.

The Criminal Justice Act 1991 will extend the availability of the live television link to youth court proceedings, and makes a number of further reforms to the law of evidence and procedure relating to child witnesses in England and Wales. The presumption that young children are not competent to give evidence in criminal proceedings is effectively removed, and video-recorded interviews will be admissible as a child witness's main evidence.

Fraud Proceedings

In England, Wales and Northern Ireland the judge in complex fraud cases may order a preparatory open Crown Court hearing to be held. This provides an opportunity for the judge to determine questions regarding admissibility of evidence and any other questions of law relating to the case. The judge also has the power to order the prosecution and the defence to serve on each other certain statements and to prepare the case in such a way that it is easier to understand. Appeals may be made to the Court of Appeal from decisions of the judge in the preparatory hearings. The law on evidence has been changed to make it possible for courts to have before them a wider range of written evidence in the form of business documents which could be relevant to a successful prosecution.

The use of information technology systems to support the investigation and prosecution of fraud cases is being improved. Within the Serious Fraud Office, a case support section has been set up whose responsibility is to determine and meet the information technology needs of each case. This work includes forensic computing (for example, the seizure of computers and securing of data for use as evidence) as well as the provision of technology to manage the large volume of material generated in fraud investigations; and the deployment of graphic techniques for the presentation of complex evidence in court.

The Jury

In jury trials the judge decides questions of law, sums up the evidence for the jury, instructs it on the relevant law and discharges the accused or passes sentence. In England, Wales and Northern Ireland the jury is responsible for deciding whether a defendant is 'guilty' or 'not guilty', the latter verdict resulting in acquittal. If the jury cannot reach a unanimous verdict, the judge may direct it to bring in a majority verdict provided that, in the normal jury of 12 people, there are not more than two dissenters.

In Scotland the jury's verdict may be 'guilty', 'not guilty' or 'not proven'; the accused is acquitted if one of the last two verdicts is given. The jury consists of 15 people and a verdict of 'guilty' can only be reached if at least eight members are in favour. As a general rule no one may be convicted without corroborated evidence.

If the jury acquits the defendant, the prosecution has no right of appeal and the defendant cannot be tried again for the same offence. The defendant, however, has a right of appeal to the appropriate court if found guilty.

A jury is independent of the judiciary. Any attempt to interfere with a jury once it is sworn in is a criminal offence. Potential jurors are put on a panel in court before the start of the trial. In England and Wales the prosecution and the defence may challenge individual jurors on the panel, giving reasons for doing so. In Scotland the prosecution or defence may also challenge up to three jurors without reason. In Northern Ireland each defendant has the right to challenge up to 12 potential jurors without giving reason.

People between the ages of 18 and 70 in England, Wales and Northern Ireland (65 in Scotland) whose names appear on the electoral register, with certain exceptions, are liable for jury service and their names are chosen at random. Ineligible people include, for example, judges and people who have within the previous ten years been members of the legal profession or the police, prison or probation services. Persons disqualified from jury service include those convicted of certain offences within the previous ten years. Anyone who has received a prison sentence of five years or more is disqualified for life.

Sentencing

If a person is convicted, the magistrate or judge (and their Scottish equivalents) decides on the most appropriate sentence. Account is taken of the facts of the offence, the circumstances of the offender and any previous convictions or sentences.

For serious offenders, a social enquiry report providing fuller information is given to the court by a probation officer (or social worker in Scotland). This gives details about the character, personality, social and domestic background of the offender, his or her education and employment record, and comments on possible sentences. Under the provisions of the Criminal Justice Act 1991, courts will have to obtain and consider a 'pre-sentence' report before imposing a custodial sentence or certain community sentences. These reports will be similar to social enquiry reports but focused more sharply on the type of sentence envisaged.

The defence lawyer may make a speech in mitigation on behalf of the offender.

Appeals

England and Wales

A person convicted by a magistrates' court may appeal to the Crown Court against the sentence imposed if he or she has pleaded guilty. An appeal may be made against both conviction and sentence if a 'not guilty' plea has been made. The Divisional Court of the Queen's Bench Division of the High Court hears appeals on points of law and procedure—by either prosecution or defence—in cases originally dealt with by magistrates. If convicted by the Crown Court, a defendant can appeal to the Court of Appeal (Criminal Division) against both the conviction and the sentence imposed. The House of Lords is the final appeal court, but it will only consider cases that involve a point of law of general public importance and where leave to appeal is granted.

The Attorney General may seek the opinion of the Court of Appeal on a point of law which has arisen in a case where a person tried on indictment is acquitted. The Court has power to refer the point to the House of Lords if necessary. The acquittal in the original case is not affected.

The Attorney General may also refer a case to the Court of Appeal if he considers that a sentence passed by the Crown Court is too lenient. This applies to a case triable only on indictment in the Crown Court. If the Court of Appeal agrees, it may increase the sentence within the statutory maximum laid down by Parliament for the offence.

The Home Secretary may consider representations and intervene in cases where appeal rights have been exhausted. The emergence of fresh evidence since a conviction is deemed necessary for such action.

Scotland

All appeal cases are dealt with by the High Court of Justiciary and are heard by at least three judges. In both solemn and summary procedure, an appeal may be brought by the accused against conviction, or sentence, or both. The Court may authorise a retrial if it sets aside a conviction. There is no further appeal to the House of Lords. In summary proceedings the prosecutor may appeal on a point of law against acquittal or sentence. The Lord Advocate may seek the opinion of the High Court on a point of law which has arisen in a case where a person tried on indictment is acquitted. The acquittal in the original case is not affected.

Northern Ireland

In Northern Ireland, appeals from magistrates' courts against conviction or sentence are heard by the county court. An appeal on a point of law alone can be heard by the Northern Ireland Court of Appeal, which also hears appeals from the Crown Court against conviction or sentence. Procedures for a further appeal to the House of Lords are similar to those in England and Wales.

Treatment of Offenders

The Government's aim is to ensure that convicted criminals are punished justly and suitably according to the seriousness of their offences. It believes that those who commit very serious crimes, particularly crimes of violence, should receive long custodial sentences, but that many other crimes can best be punished within the community through compensation and reparation. These principles are contained in the Criminal Justice Act 1991.

Legislation sets the maximum penalties for offences, the sentence being entirely a matter for the courts subject to these maxima. The Court of Appeal issues guidance to the lower courts on sentencing issues when points of principle have arisen on individual cases which are the subject of appeal.

In Scotland, where many offences are not created by statute, the penalty for offences at common law range from absolute discharge to life imprisonment.

Custody

England and Wales
Imprisonment is the most severe penalty ordinarily available to the courts. The Government believes that custody should be used only for offenders convicted of serious criminal offences or where the public needs to be protected from a violent or sexual offender.

The Court of Appeal has stated that sentencers in England and Wales should ensure that terms of custody are as short as possible, consistent with the courts' duty to protect the public and to punish and deter the criminal.

The Criminal Justice Act 1991 will require a court in England and Wales, before giving a custodial sentence, to be satisfied that the offence is serious enough to merit custody. The court will also have to give reasons, in cases other than those where the sentence for the offence is fixed by law, if it considers a custodial sentence to be necessary. Longer custodial sentences—within the statutory limits—will be available for persistent violent and sexual offenders in order to protect the public from serious harm.

A magistrates' court in England and Wales cannot impose a term of more than six months' imprisonment for an individual offence tried summarily. It can impose consecutive sentences for 'either way' offences (see p. 31), subject to an overall maximum of 12 months' imprisonment. If an offence carries a higher maximum penalty, the court may commit the offender for sentence at the Crown Court.

For an offence deemed sufficiently serious to justify a prison sentence of not more than two years, a court may decide that the operation of that sentence should be fully suspended. A sentence within this range may be suspended for an 'operational period' of at least one year and not more than two years. The suspended prison term is not served unless the offender commits another imprisonable offence during the period of suspension. The suspended sentence is then normally served in addition to any punishment imposed for the second offence. The court may also order supervision of the offender by a probation officer if the suspended sentence is one of more than six months. A sentence can also be partly suspended but this provision is being abolished by the Criminal Justice Act 1991.

There is a mandatory sentence of life imprisonment for murder throughout Britain. Life imprisonment is also the maximum penalty for a number of serious offences such as robbery, rape, arson and manslaughter.

Scotland and Northern Ireland

In trials on indictment in Scotland the High Court of Justiciary may impose a sentence of imprisonment for any term up to life, and the sheriff court any term up to three years. The latter may send any person to the High Court for sentence if the court considers its powers are insufficient. In summary cases, the sheriff or stipendiary magistrate may normally impose up to three months' imprisonment or six months' for some repeated offences. The district court can impose a maximum term of imprisonment of 60 days.

In Northern Ireland the position is generally the same as for England and Wales. A magistrates' court, however, cannot commit an offender for sentencing at the Crown Court if it has tried the case.

The Death Penalty

The death penalty has been repealed for almost all offences. It remains on the statute book for the offences of treason, piracy with violence and some other treasonable and mutinous offences. It has, however, not been used for any of these offences since 1946.

Police helicopter on patrol over central London.

The CAD (computer-aided despatch) room in a police station: upon receipt of information, officers are directed to the scene of the crime.

Reconstruction of an identity parade at Kilburn Police Station, London.

Officers from Kilburn Police Station visit a school to explain their work.

A court clerk advising magistrates at Uxbridge, London.

A senior clerk at work at Leicester Magistrates' Court.

Reconstruction of a witness being sworn in at a Crown Court.

Offenders making equipment for a children's playscheme in an inner-city area as part of a community service order.

Probation officers encourage offenders to develop skills required by employers.

Staff and inmates at Cookham Wood Prison, Kent.

Supervising a women's prison workshop.

Inmates working in the gardens of Maghaberry Prison, Northern Ireland.

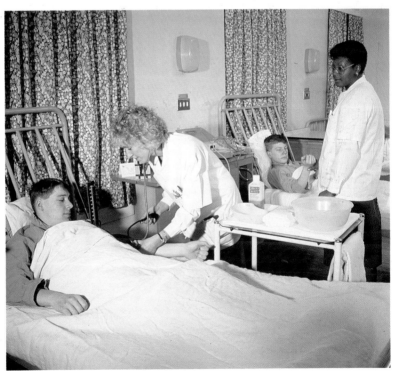

Tending inmates at Rochester Prison Hospital.

A prison officer at Belmarsh Prison, which opened in July 1991.

Non-Custodial Treatment

The Government believes that more offenders, particularly those convicted of property crimes and less serious cases of violence, should be punished in the community. In its view this should involve probation, community service and fines levied on the offender and compensation to the victim.

Fines

A court may fine an offender for any offence, except murder or treason. A fine enables the court to demonstrate society's disapproval of an offence in a case where punishment (short of custody) is the appropriate response. About 80 per cent of offenders are punished with a financial penalty. A court may impose a fine as an alternative to custody, but at present it may not be combined for the same offence with a discharge, probation order or community service order (see p. 47). For most imprisonable offences a court may impose a fine as well as custody or a suspended sentence.

There is no limit to the fine, unless set by statute, which the Crown Court (and High Court of Justiciary in Scotland) may impose on indictment. On summary conviction the maximum limit is usually £2,000 in England, Wales and Northern Ireland, and in Scotland £2,000 in the sheriff court and £1,000 in the district court.

The Criminal Justice Act 1991 will enable fines to be more closely related to ability to pay, through the application of a unit fine system in magistrates' courts in England and Wales. The court's sentence will be given in units reflecting the seriousness of the offence, and the value of each unit settled according to the offender's disposable weekly income. Courts will be empowered to require offenders to supply statements about their income. The maximum fine usually available on summary conviction will be increased to £5,000. Any period of imprisonment imposed in default of payment of a unit fine will be related to the number of units rather than the amount of the fine.

Probation

The Probation Service is administered locally in England and Wales by committees of magistrates and community representatives. It supervises offenders in the community, both under direct court orders and after release from custody, and also provides offenders in custody with help and advice.

A probation order can last between six months and three years. It can only be made by a court with the consent of the offender, who may be sentenced for the original offence if he or she fails to comply with the order or commits another offence while on probation.

The most basic probation order requires that the offender must maintain regular contact with his or her probation officer and notify any change of address. The court expects the probation officer to supervise the offender during the probation period.

Probation orders with additional requirements all make more demands and take away more of the offender's liberty. For example, special conditions attached to the order may require the offender to attend a day centre for up to 60 days. Day centre staff work with groups and individual offenders who are made to face up to the consequences of their actions, and to consider both the circumstances of their offending behaviour and the effects it has had on other people. Day centre programmes aim to help offenders make recompense and tackle problems which stand in the way of their becoming law-abiding citizens.

Although intended as a punishment, the time spent by offenders under supervision in the community offers an opportunity for constructive work to reduce the likelihood of re-offending. The flexibility of the probation order means that probation is suitable for those convicted of offences of differing degrees of seriousness.

In England and Wales the probation service also administers supervision orders (see p. 65), the community service scheme and supervises those released from prison on parole.

Under the Criminal Justice Act 1991 in England and Wales, a probation order will become a sentence of the court (at present it is imposed 'instead of sentencing'), enabling it to be used in combination with a community service order or a fine for a single offence. Her Majesty's Inspectorate of Probation is to be put on a statutory basis under the same legislation. It will monitor the work of the voluntary and private sectors with the probation service in addition to its existing inspection and advisory duties. National objectives and standards are to be introduced for a wide range of probation work.

In Scotland there is no separate probation service. The supervision of offenders on probation, supervision order or parole is the responsibility of local authority social work services.

In Northern Ireland the service is administered by a probation board, whose membership is representative of the community and which is funded by central government.

Community Service

Offenders aged 16 or over convicted of imprisonable offences may, with their consent, be given community service orders. The aim of community service is both punitive and reparative. The court may order between 40 and 240 hours' unpaid service to be completed within 12 months; for 16-year-olds in England and Wales the present maximum of 120 hours is to be raised to the same level as that for adults (see p. 67).

The order is carried out under the direction of a community service organiser working within the probation service. Examples of work done include decorating the houses of elderly or disabled people and building adventure playgrounds. It is usually done in spells of several hours on one day a week.

National standards for community service orders were introduced in April 1989 to ensure that all orders meet a common set of minimum requirements—for example, that the offender starts work within 10 days, that lateness will be treated as failure to attend and that detailed records of attendance are kept. If an offender fails to comply with a community service order 'without reasonable excuse', the community service organiser may apply for a summons or warrant and the offender is brought before the magistrates' court. If the court is satisfied that the offender has failed to carry out the order, it may either:

—order the offender to pay a fine of up to £400, and let the order remain in force; or

—revoke the order, and re-sentence the offender for the original offence.

The Criminal Justice Act 1991 will introduce a new court order in England and Wales—the combination order—combining elements of community service and probation supervision. The maximum term for the probation element will be the same as a probation order and the maximum period of community service will be 100 hours. The combination order will impose a significant restriction on the liberty of the offender.

Curfew Order

Under the same legislation, courts in England and Wales will be empowered to issue a curfew order confining offenders to specified places at specified times in order to avoid circumstances which have led them to offend before. It can also be combined with probation, community service or the new combination order. The enforcement of curfew orders may be assisted by the inclusion of a requirement for the electronic monitoring of the offender's whereabouts.

Compensation and Reparation

The courts may order an offender to pay compensation for personal injury, loss or damage resulting from an offence. A compensation order may be the only sentence for the offence, or it may be made in addition to any other sentence (including a probation order or discharge) which the court thinks appropriate, except a criminal bankruptcy order. Courts in England and Wales are required to give reasons for not awarding compensation to a victim.

When a court considers both a compensation order and a fine to be appropriate, preference is given to compensation if the offender's means are insufficient to pay both in full. A compensation order also takes precedence in the procedures for enforcing payment by offenders of compensation, fines or orders to pay prosecution costs.

The making of a compensation order enables the victim to obtain speedy redress without having to institute civil proceedings, and allows the court to impress directly on the offender the harm done to the victim. The Crown Court may award any amount of compensation, up to the amount of the loss, damage or injury; the magistrates' court may award up to £2,000 for any one offence. Compensation ordered by a court is different from compensation payable by the Criminal Injuries Compensation Board in England and Wales (see p. 10).

Courts may order the confiscation of proceeds gained by a criminal from drug trafficking and other offences such as robbery, fraud, blackmail and insider dealing in shares.

Other Measures

A court in England and Wales may discharge a person if it believes that punishment should not be inflicted and that a probation order is not appropriate. An absolute discharge is used where the court, having found the offender guilty of the offence charged, considers that no further action is required on its part beyond the finding of guilt. An order for conditional discharge similarly imposes no obligation on the offender, but he or she remains liable to punishment for the offence if convicted of another offence within a period specified by the court (not more than three years).

The Crown Court may 'bind over' an offender. This means that the offender recognises that a failure to comply with certain conditions stated by the court will mean the forfeiture of a sum of money. The court may also require the offender to keep the peace and/or be of good behaviour. If this requirement is not complied with, the money may be forfeited and the offender brought before the court and dealt with for the original offence. Magistrates' courts also have powers to 'bind over'.

In Scotland there is a system of deferral of sentence until a future date. During this period the accused is required to be of good behaviour and to meet any other conditions stipulated by the court. The court may also warn the offender or grant an absolute discharge.

Police cautions are used particularly for young offenders. The caution is a form of warning and no court action is taken.

Costs of the Prosecution
A defendant who is convicted of an offence may be ordered to pay the prosecutor such costs as the court considers just and reasonable. The amount to be paid should be specified by the court.

Prisons
The Prison Service in England and Wales is managed directly by the Home Office, with funding of £1,300 million in 1991–92. Scotland and Northern Ireland have separate prison services run by the Scottish and Northern Ireland Offices.

The average prison population in 1990 was about 45,600 inmates in England and Wales, 4,739 in Scotland and 1,750 in Northern Ireland. Prisoners may be housed in accommodation ranging from open prisons to high security establishments. In England, Scotland and Wales sentenced prisoners are classified into groups for security purposes. There are separate prisons for women. There are no open prisons in Northern Ireland, where the majority of offenders are serving sentences for terrorist offences. People awaiting trial in custody are entitled to privileges not granted to convicted prisoners. Those under 21 are, where possible, separated from convicted prisoners.

Many prisons in Great Britain were built in the nineteenth century and require major repairs to bring them up to modern standards. In order to ensure that all prisoners are housed in decent conditions, a major programme of improvement is in progress which will, in England and Wales for example, eliminate cells without access to integral sanitation. Overcrowding is being relieved by a prison building programme. In Northern Ireland there is no overcrowding in the four prisons and one young offenders' centre. Four of these establishments have been built since 1972.

The incorporation of integral sanitation and other major improvements to the prison estate are under way in Scotland, where, with a few localised exceptions, overcrowding is not a problem.

White Paper on the Prison Service in England and Wales

Despite the programme of prison improvement, serious disturbances occurred in April 1990 at a number of establishments in England and Wales, particularly Strangeways prison in Manchester, prompting an official inquiry into the prison system. Building on the recommendations of the consequent Woolf Report, the Government published a White Paper in September 1991, setting out a programme of reforms for the Prison Service in England and Wales and focusing on the key areas of custody, care and justice.

The White Paper confirmed the Government's acceptance of the central propositions in the Woolf Report—that security and control must be kept in balance with justice and humanity and that each must be set at the right level. The aim is to provide a better prison system, with more effective measures for security and control, more constructive relationships between prisoners and staff and more stimulating and useful programmes for prisoners. A priority programme set out in the White Paper is summarised below:

Security and Control—The White Paper announced the installation of X-ray search machines in 23 prisons, together with annual security audits and the issue of security and contingency planning manuals in all establishments. A new offence of prison mutiny has been introduced, whereby the maximum penalty for assisting a prisoner to escape increases to ten years' imprisonment.

Delegation and Leadership—The Prison Service will remain directly accountable to ministers, with clear delegation to governors of establishments. The proposals included the publication, in May of each year, of a 'compact' between the Home Secretary and the Director General of the Prison Service, setting out the annual objectives and the resources available to the Service.

Staff—Recognising the staff of the Prison Service as its most valuable asset, the White Paper proposed to enhance the nature and range of the work of prison officers and to improve training. It also highlighted the need to change industrial relations in the Prison Service. The number of prison officers working in establishments has increased by about 4,000 (20 per cent) since 1987.

Remand Prisoners—The White Paper said that the Prison Rules should be revised so that separate rules apply to unconvicted prisoners on remand, reflecting their particular legal status. Regimes in local prisons and remand centres are to be improved.

Active Prison Regimes—The Government acknowledged the need to provide as full a programme of activities and opportunities for prisoners as the available resources allowed, covering work, access to education and training (see p. 60), links with the family and programmes for certain groups of prisoners, such as sex offenders.

Code of Standards—Recognising the obligation to provide prisoners with decent as well as secure conditions, the White Paper proposed the introduction of a code of standards on the provision of services to prisoners, encompassing food, clothing, hygiene and health care.

Relations with Prisoners—The White Paper envisaged increased consultation with prisoners on general issues affecting their daily lives. It also proposed the introduction of 'prisoner compacts' or statements of the facilities available for prisoners and what is expected of them in return. An independent appeal body, a Complaints Adjudicator, would be established to consider disciplinary cases and prisoner complaints which had exhausted normal procedures within the Prison Service. Boards of Visitors (see p. 59) would consequently be relieved of their disciplinary powers.

Sanitation—The Government intends to ensure that all prisoners have access to sanitation at all times by the end of 1994. During 1991–92, 4,000 sanitation systems are being installed and 5,000 new places with full sanitation are coming into use in new and refurbished prisons.

Overcrowding—Through an extensive building programme, providing for 21 new prisons, the Government is planning to eliminate overcrowded accommodation in prisons by the middle of the 1990s. During 1991–92, 3,700 places are being provided in new prisons in addition to 700 new places at existing establishments.

Small Prison Units—The White Paper favoured the division of large wings in existing prisons into smaller units with better security. All new prisons are being built with secure living units for between 50 and 70 prisoners.

Community Prisons—Recognising the advantage of locating prisoners near to their homes, the White Paper proposed that the Prison Service should identify a number of new and existing prisons which could be converted to multi-functional community prisons and other prisons to be grouped into community clusters.

Scotland

Many of these policies are common to Scotland. The Scottish Prison Service has published various documents setting out its strategy for the future, in particular on encouraging prisoners to take more responsibility for planning their sentences and on reorganising the service.

Private Sector Involvement

The Government is seeking to foster greater private sector involvement in the prison system of England and Wales. Under the Criminal Justice Act 1991 the Home Secretary is empowered to contract out the management of prisons and to allow escort and guarding functions to be carried out by the private sector. A new remand centre, the Wolds, has come into use under private management, and it is proposed to invite tenders for the management of Blakenhurst local prison, which is due to open early in 1993.

In order to extend the range of prison work available to inmates, the Government is considering the introduction of pilot schemes to increase the involvement of private employers.

Remission of Sentence

Most prisoners in Great Britain are currently eligible for remission of one-third of their sentence. Prisoners serving a sentence of 12 months or less in England and Wales are entitled to half-remission. Release on remission does not involve any official supervision in the community. It may be forfeited for serious misconduct in prison.

In Northern Ireland prisoners serving a sentence of more than five days are eligible for remission of half their sentence. A prisoner serving a sentence of more than 12 months who is given remission is liable to be ordered to serve the remainder of this sentence if convicted of fresh imprisonable offences during this period. The rate of remission for those convicted of terrorist offences since 1989 and serving sentences of five years or more is one-third. Any released prisoners convicted of another terrorist offence before the expiry of the original sentence must complete that sentence before serving any term for the second offence.

Parole

At present, prisoners in England and Wales serving sentences of more than 12 months can be conditionally released on parole when they have served one-third of the sentence, or six months, whichever expires the later. In Scotland they qualify on completion of one-third of the sentence or one year, whichever is the longer.

The first stage of the parole procedure in England and Wales is consideration by a local review committee attached to each prison. This is followed by scrutiny by Home Office officials, who refer the more difficult and complex cases to the Parole Board. The Board makes recommendations for release on parole and

Home Office ministers take the final decision on whether to accept the recommendation. Less serious cases are dealt with by the Home Office without reference to the Board on the basis of the local review committee recommendation. A similar procedure operates in Scotland, where there is a separate Parole Board.

Of those cases reviewed in England and Wales each year, three quarters of prisoners serving sentences of less than two years receive parole; the corresponding figure for those serving two years or more is about one half. Parole is only granted in exceptional circumstances, or for a few months at the end of sentence, for those serving sentences of over five years for violence, arson, sexual offences or drug trafficking. The parole licence remains in force until the date on which the prisoner would otherwise have been released from prison. It prescribes the conditions, including contact with a supervising officer, with which the offender must comply.

Parole is not available in Northern Ireland because of the more generous remission terms.

New Legislation

Upon the entry into force in England and Wales of the Criminal Justice Act 1991, the current system of remission of sentence and parole will be replaced with new arrangements for the early release of prisoners, and for their supervision and liabilities after release. The Parole Board will continue to advise the Home Secretary on the early release or recall of long-term prisoners.

Prisoners serving terms of less than four years will be released once they have served half of their sentences. Long-term prisoners (those serving more than four years) will be released once they have served two-thirds of their sentence, although the legislation provides for the discretionary release on licence by the Home Secretary, on the recommendation of the Parole Board, of long-term prisoners once they have served half of their sentence. All prisoners sentenced to a year or more will be supervised on release until three-quarters of their sentence has passed. Certain sex offenders may be supervised to the end of their sentence.

If convicted of another offence punishable with imprisonment and committed before the end of the original sentence, a released prisoner will be liable to serve all or part of the original sentence outstanding at the time the fresh offence was committed.

Similar changes are to be made in Scotland.

Life Sentence Prisoners
Under the Criminal Justice Act 1991, new procedures will operate in England and Wales for the release of life sentence prisoners convicted for offences other than murder. The Home Secretary will be required to release such prisoners after an initial period set by the trial judge if so directed by the Parole Board, who will have to be satisfied that the protection of the public does not require their further confinement. These new provisions conform with the requirements of the European Convention on Human Rights. Similar procedures are to be introduced in Scotland.

People serving life sentences for the murder of police and prison officers, terrorist murders, murder by firearms in the course of robbery and the sexual or sadistic murder of children are normally detained for at least 20 years. The release on licence of prisoners serving mandatory life sentences for murder may only be authorised by the Home Secretary on the recommendation of the Parole Board. A similar policy applies in Scotland.

At the end of 1991 there were about 3,000 life sentence prisoners detained in prisons in England and Wales, of whom about 270 had been detained for over 15 years. The equivalent figures in Scotland were 437 and 31 respectively.

On release, life sentence prisoners remain on licence for the rest of their lives and are subject to recall should their behaviour suggest that they might again be a danger to the public.

In Northern Ireland the Secretary of State reviews life sentence cases on the recommendation of an internal review body.

Repatriation

Sentenced prisoners who are nationals of countries which have ratified the Council of Europe Convention on the Transfer of Sentenced Persons or similar international arrangements may apply to be returned to their own country to serve the rest of their sentence there.

Independent Oversight of the Prison System

Every prison establishment has a Board of Visitors—a Visiting Committee in Scotland—drawn from the local community, which acts as a watchdog for the Secretary of State. These bodies oversee prison administration and the treatment of prisoners. In order to see that prisoners are being treated fairly, members may go to any part of the prison and interview any inmate at any time. Except in Scotland, these bodies also adjudicate on prisoners who have committed the more serious offences against prison discipline.

The White Paper on the Prison Service in England and Wales recommended that Boards of Visitors should relinquish their adjudicatory role, allowing them to strengthen their central function as watch-dogs of the prison system.

The independent Prisons Inspectorates report to the respective Secretaries of State on the treatment of prisoners and prison conditions. The Chief Inspector publishes reports of inspections and annual reports in which he is free to make criticisms. Each establishment is visited about every two years.

Prison Industries, Education and Physical Education

Prison industries aim to give inmates work experience which will assist them when released and to secure a return which will reduce the cost of the prison system. The main industries are clothing and textile manufacture, engineering, woodwork, laundering, farming and horticulture, and printing. In England and Wales most prison production caters for internal needs and for other public services, whereas in Scotland a greater proportion is sold to the private sector.

A few prisoners are employed outside prison, some in community service projects. Inmates are paid at pocket money rates for work done; in some prisons incentive payment schemes provide an opportunity for higher earnings on the basis of output and skill.

Education is financed by the prison service and staffed by local education authorities. Full-time education of 15 hours a week is compulsory for young offenders below school-leaving age. The aim is to ensure that education and training undertaken while in custody are compatible with an inmate's previous experience and with general provision in the community. For older offenders education is voluntary. Some prisoners study for public examinations, including those of the Open University.

The Prison Service in England and Wales is placing increasing emphasis on the development and implementation of National

Vocational Qualifications[3] for inmates. A full-time co-ordinator and supporting team for National Vocational Qualifications have been appointed to encourage the introduction of these qualifications in all establishments across a wide range of activities. Similar moves are under way in Scotland.

All new prisons have purpose-built education units and schemes to build new education accommodation or to refurbish or extend existing facilities are also under way or planned at many other establishments.

Physical education is voluntary for adult offenders but compulsory for young offenders. Practically all prisons have physical education facilities, some of which are purpose built. Opportunities are given for inmates to obtain proficiency awards issued by governing bodies of sport. Inmates also compete against teams in the local community.

Medical and Psychiatric Care

The Health Care Service for Prisoners in England and Wales is responsible for the physical and mental health of all those in custody. It was launched in April 1992 following a 1990 efficiency scrutiny of the prison medical service which proposed greater emphasis on health promotion and prevention of illness.

A review of services for mentally disordered offenders is being undertaken jointly by the Department of Health and the Home Office; this has already resulted in the provision of another 400 medium-secure psychiatric beds. A Health Advisory Committee provides independent medical advice on prisoners to government

[3] A system of accreditation for qualifications awarded for various levels of occupational competence by approved bodies.

ministers, the Prison Service Director General and the Director of Health Care.

Privileges and Discipline

Prisoners may write and receive letters and be visited by relatives and friends, and those in some establishments may make telephone calls. Privileges include a personal radio, books, periodicals and newspapers, and the opportunity to make purchases from the canteen with money earned in prison. Depending on facilities, prisoners may be granted the further privileges of dining and recreation with other inmates, and watching television.

Breaches of discipline are dealt with by the prison governor or, except in Scotland, by the Board of Visitors. The Government has proposed in the White Paper that prison governors should in future conduct all disciplinary cases within their current powers and that there should be an appeal system to an independent body against decisions arising from the disciplinary and complaints procedures (see p. 54).

Welfare

Prison officers deal with welfare matters and are supported in this by probation staff (or social workers in Scotland), who use their own professional skills to help individual prisoners understand more about the nature of their offending behaviour.

Religion and Spiritual Care

Anglican, Church of Scotland, Roman Catholic and Methodist chaplains provide opportunities for worship and spiritual counselling. They are supported by visiting ministers of other denominations and faiths as required. In a multi-faith and multicultural society particular attention is given to the needs of those of non-Christian faiths and ethnic minorities.

Preparation for Release

The Prison Service has a duty to prepare prisoners for release. Sentence planning is being extended progressively to all prisoners serving substantial sentences, in conjunction with extended arrangements for aftercare (see below). Many medium- and long-term prisoners in the later parts of their sentences may be granted home leave for short periods. Its purpose is to to give the prisoner the opportunity to re-establish links with family and friends, and, where leave is taken near the end of the sentence, to contact prospective employers and make firm plans for release.

The Pre-Release Employment Scheme provides an opportunity for selected long-term prisoners to spend their last six months before release in certain hostels attached to prisons, in order to help them re-adapt to society. Hostellers work in the outside community and return to the hostel each evening. Frequent weekend leave allows hostellers to renew ties with their families.

In Northern Ireland arrangements exist for prisoners serving fixed sentences to have short periods of leave near the end of their sentences and at Christmas. Life-sentence prisoners are given a nine-month pre-release programme which includes employment outside the prison.

Aftercare

Professional social work support is given to offenders following their release. Most young offenders under the age of 22, adult offenders released on parole and those released on licence from a life sentence receive a period of compulsory supervision from the probation service.

Voluntary organisations which exist to help offenders include the National Association for the Care and Resettlement of Offenders which:

—runs housing, employment, education and other practical resettlement projects for ex-offenders and others;

—works with other agencies locally and nationally to develop new approaches to tackling crime and dealing with offenders;

—provides information and training services for individuals and for agencies working with ex-offenders; and

—develops and promotes policies for improving the criminal justice system.

Young Offenders

England and Wales

In England and Wales criminal proceedings cannot be brought against children below the age of 10 years. Children aged between 10 and 16 are currently brought before a juvenile court if charged with a criminal offence. If a child is found guilty, the court may:

—grant a conditional or absolute discharge (see p. 50);

—order payment of compensation;

—impose a fine which the parents can be ordered to pay;

—impose a supervision order or attendance centre order;

—impose a community service order (for 16-year-olds) for up to 120 hours; or

—in some cases, pass a custodial sentence.

Since October 1991, when the Children Act 1989 came into force, child care orders (under which children become the responsibility of local government social services) can no longer be used as a disposal in criminal cases and juvenile courts can no longer hear care proceedings.

Non-Custodial Treatment

Under a supervision order, which may remain in force up to a maximum of three years, a child normally lives at home under the supervision of a social worker or a probation officer. The order can be used to provide for a programme of constructive and remedial activities by means of a short residential course or, more usually, attendance at a day or evening centre. The court can decide what requirements to make by including them in the order, or it can delegate authority to the supervisor.

Anyone under 21 years of age who is found guilty of an offence for which an adult may be imprisoned can be ordered to attend at an attendance centre for a number of hours. An attendance centre order may also be made where the offender has not complied with another order (for example, failure to pay a fine or breach of a probation order).

The maximum total number of hours of attendance is 36 (or 24 if the offender is aged under 17) and the minimum is 12 hours. The order is served by attending the centre on several different occasions, the longest period of attendance in any one day being three hours. The aim of the order is to encourage offenders, while in a disciplined environment, to make more constructive use of their leisure time.

Attendance centres are a locally based provision run in most cases by police officers. Officers in charge of centres have discretion to develop the regime to suit the local conditions and the needs and aptitudes of the offenders sent to them.

Custody

The criteria for imposing a custodial sentence on a young offender are that:

—only a custodial sentence will adequately protect the public from serious harm from the offender; or

—the offence is so serious that a non-custodial sentence cannot be justified.

Boys aged between 14 and 16 may be sent to a young offender institution. For those aged 14 the maximum period is four months and for those aged 15 or 16 it is 12 months. This sentence is also available for girls from the age of 15. In the case of a very serious crime, detention in a place approved by the Home Secretary may be ordered, and must be ordered in the case of murder.

The custodial sentence for those aged between 17 and 20 years is also detention in a young offender institution. The use of custody for this group has dropped by 40 per cent since 1985. Alternative penalties include fines and compensation, attendance centre orders (for up to 36 hours) and community service orders (for between 40 and 240 hours).

The period served in a young offender institution may be reduced, through remission and parole, in the same way as the period served under a sentence of imprisonment (see p. 56). An offender sentenced to detention in a young offender institution is normally subject to statutory supervision on release from custody. The length of the period of supervision, usually between three and 12 months, depends on the length of the sentence and the age of the offender. Failure to comply with the requirements of this supervision is punishable by a fine or a custodial sentence of not more than 30 days.

Changes in the Law

When the Criminal Justice Act 1991 enters into force, it will make major changes in the arrangements for dealing with young offenders in England and Wales. In future, 17-year-olds will be brought within the jurisdiction of juvenile courts, which will be renamed youth courts. For 16-year-olds the maximum length of a community service order will be extended to 240 hours, and that for an attendance centre order to 36 hours—in line with the arrangements for 17-year-olds. In addition, probation orders, supervision orders and the new combination and curfew orders will be available for 16- and 17-year-olds. Detention in a young offender institution for 14-year-old boys is being abolished, in line with existing disposals for girls of that age.

The new legislation makes provision for the courts to remand juveniles, who need to be held in secure conditions while awaiting trial or sentence, to local authority secure accommodation instead of adult prisons. Applications for children to be held in secure accommodation for more than 72 hours must be heard by a juvenile or magistrates' court.

Scotland

In Scotland the age of criminal responsibility is eight years but prosecution of children under the age of 16 is rare. Children under 16 who have committed an offence or are considered to be in need of care and protection may be brought before a children's panel, which consists of three lay people. This children's hearing determines in an informal setting whether compulsory measures of care are required and, if so, the form they should take. An official 'reporter' decides whether a child should come before a hearing. If the grounds for referral are not accepted by the child or parent, the case goes to the sheriff for proof. If the sheriff finds the grounds established, the case is remitted to the reporter to arrange a hearing. The sheriff also decides appeals against any decision of a children's hearing.

Custody is available to the courts for young people aged between 16 and 21; as in England and Wales they serve their sentence in a young offender institution. Remission of part of the sentence for good behaviour, release on parole and supervision on release are available.

Northern Ireland

Children between the ages of 10 and 13 and young persons between the ages of 14 and 16 who are charged with a criminal offence will normally be brought before a juvenile court. If found guilty of an offence punishable in the case of an adult by imprisonment, the court may order the child or young person to be placed in care, under supervision or on probation. The offender may also be required to attend a day attendance centre, be sent to a training school or committed to custody in a remand home. Non-custodial options are the same as in England and Wales.

Offenders aged between 17 and 21 who receive custodial sentences of less than three years serve them in a young offenders' centre.

Administration of the Law

Government Responsibilities

Administration of criminal justice rests with the Lord Chancellor, the Home Secretary, the Attorney General and the Secretaries of State for Scotland and Northern Ireland. The highest judicial appointments are made by the Queen on the advice of the Prime Minister. The judiciary is independent, its adjudications not being subject to ministerial direction or control.

England and Wales

The Lord Chancellor is concerned with court procedure and is responsible for the administration of the criminal courts and, from 1 April 1992, for the finance, management and organisation of the magistrates' courts. He recommends judicial appointments to the Crown, appoints magistrates, and has general responsibility for the legal aid and advice schemes.

The Home Secretary is responsible for the police service, prisons, and the probation and after-care service. He appoints a Board of Visitors to each prison establishment (see p. 59) and is advised by the Parole Board on the release of prisoners on licence. The Home Secretary is also responsible for advising the Queen on the exercise of the royal prerogative of mercy to pardon a person convicted of a crime or to remit all or part of a penalty imposed by a court.

The Attorney General and the Solicitor General are the Government's principal advisers on English law, and they represent the Crown in appropriate domestic and international cases. They are senior barristers, elected members of the House of Commons and hold ministerial posts. The Attorney General, who is also Attorney General for Northern Ireland, has final responsibility for enforcing the criminal law. The Solicitor General is, in effect, the deputy of the Attorney General. As head of the Crown Prosecution Service, the Director of Public Prosecutions is subject to superintendance by the Attorney General, as are the Director of Public Prosecutions for Northern Ireland and the Director of the Serious Fraud Office.

In pursuit of greater co-operation within the criminal justice system, there are regular contacts at ministerial and official level between the Home Office, the Lord Chancellor's Department and the Attorney General's Office. In addition, government departments meet regularly with the representative organisations for the various services, for the magistrates' courts and for the legal profession. There is also a developing pattern of regional and local liaison arrangements between the criminal justice services.

The Government has established the Criminal Justice Consultative Council as a national forum to promote better understanding, co-operation and co-ordination in the criminal justice system. Area committees are being established to improve local co-ordination.

The Home Office Research and Planning Unit provides a research and advice service to the Home Office on issues relevant to policy and planning, including the criminal justice system.

Scotland

The Secretary of State for Scotland recommends the appointment of all judges other than the most senior ones, appoints the staff of the High Court of Justiciary, and is responsible for the composition, staffing and organisation of the sheriff courts. District courts are staffed and administered by the local districts and islands authorities.

The Secretary of State is responsible for crime prevention matters, the police, the penal system and legal aid. He is advised on parole matters by the Parole Board for Scotland.

The Lord Advocate and the Solicitor General for Scotland are the chief legal advisers to the Government on Scottish questions and the principal representatives of the Crown for the purposes of litigation. Both are government ministers. The Lord Advocate is closely concerned with legal policy and administration and is responsible for the Scottish parliamentary counsel. He must exercise an independent discretion when prosecuting crime.

Northern Ireland

The administration of all criminal and civil courts is the responsibility of the Lord Chancellor, while the Northern Ireland Office, under the Secretary of State, deals with the criminal law, the police and the penal system. The Lord Chancellor has general responsibility for legal aid, advice and assistance.

Personnel of the Law

The courts of the United Kingdom are the Queen's Courts, since the Crown is the historic source of all judicial power. The Queen, acting on the advice of ministers, is responsible for all appointments to the judiciary.

Judges

Judges are normally appointed from practising barristers, advocates (in Scotland), or solicitors (see below).

Lay magistrates in England and Wales need no legal qualifications but are trained to give them sufficient knowledge of the law, including the rules of evidence, and of the nature and purpose of sentencing.

The Scottish district court justices of the peace need no legal qualifications, but they too must take part in training.

In Northern Ireland members of a lay panel who serve in juvenile courts undertake training courses. Resident magistrates are drawn from practising solicitors or barristers.

The Legal Profession

The legal profession is divided into two branches: barristers (advocates in Scotland) and solicitors. Barristers and advocates are known collectively as the 'Bar', and collectively and individually as 'counsel'. Solicitors undertake legal business for individual and corporate clients, while barristers and advocates advise on legal problems submitted through solicitors and present cases in the higher courts. Certain functions are common to both branches, for example, presentation of cases in the lower courts. Although people are free to conduct their own cases most people prefer to be legally represented, especially in the more serious cases.

Legal Aid in Criminal Proceedings

A person in need of legal advice or legal representation in court may qualify for help with the costs out of public funds, either free or with a contribution according to means.

In criminal proceedings in England, Wales and Northern Ireland a legal aid certificate may be granted by the court if it appears to be in the interests of justice and if a defendant is considered to require assistance in meeting his or her costs. A certificate must be granted (subject to means) when a person is committed for trial on a murder charge or where the prosecutor appeals or applies for leave to appeal from the Court of Appeal to the House of Lords. No person who is unrepresented can be given a custodial sentence for the first time unless he or she has been given the opportunity to apply for legal aid and has refused to do so, or legal aid has been refused on financial grounds.

The Legal Aid Board in England and Wales makes arrangements for duty solicitors to be present at magistrates' courts to provide initial advice and representation to unrepresented defendants. Solicitors are available, on a 24-hour basis, to give advice and assistance to suspects at police stations. The services of a solicitor at a police station and the duty solicitor at court are free.

In Northern Ireland a voluntary duty solicitor scheme has been introduced at the principal magistrates' court in Belfast. Legal aid for criminal cases in Northern Ireland is free; the assisted person is not required to make any contributions towards the cost of his or her representation.

Scotland

In Scotland, legal aid in criminal proceedings is available to all persons in custody on their first appearance in the sheriff courts and the district courts without enquiry into the person's means. Thereafter (or if the person has been cited to attend the court and is not in custody) a person seeking legal aid must apply to the Scottish Legal Aid Board. The Board assesses all applications for legal aid in summary criminal cases and must be satisfied that the costs of the case cannot be met by the applicant without undue hardship, and that it is in the interests of justice that legal aid is awarded.

In solemn proceedings the Court determines whether legal aid is to be available and must be satisfied only that the accused cannot meet the costs of the defence without undue financial hardship. Where legal aid is granted to the accused in criminal proceedings, he or she is not required to pay any contribution towards expenses (in contrast to the legally aided litigant in civil proceedings).

Royal Commission on Criminal Justice

On 14 March 1991 the Home Secretary and Lord Chancellor announced the setting up of a Royal Commission, under the chairmanship of Lord Runciman of Doxford, to inquire into the criminal investigation, prosecution and appeal processes in England and Wales.

This action was taken immediately following the decision by the Court of Appeal to quash the convictions of six men for murder arising from the bombing of two public houses in Birmingham in 1974. The Government acknowledged that this case, and other miscarriages of justice which had recently come to light, were a cause for concern and undermined public confidence in the arrangements for criminal justice. One of the main aims of the review is to minimise as far as possible the likelihood of such events happening again.

Terms of Reference

The Royal Commission will 'examine the effectiveness of the criminal justice system in England and Wales in securing the conviction of those guilty of criminal offences and the acquittal of those who are innocent'. It will consider whether changes are needed in:

—the conduct of police investigations and their supervision and control by senior police officers, particularly the degree of control over the gathering and preparation of evidence;

—the role of the prosecutor in supervising the gathering of evidence and deciding whether to proceed with a case, and the arrangements for the disclosure of material to the defence;

—the role and responsibilities of experts in criminal proceedings, and the relationship between the forensic science services and the police;

—the arrangements for the defence of accused persons and access to legal advice and expert evidence;

—the opportunities available for an accused person to state his position on the matters charged and the extent to which the courts might draw proper inferences from primary facts, the conduct of the accused, and any failure on his part to take advantage of an opportunity to state his position;

—the conduct of trials and the duties and powers of the courts, and the possibility of their having an investigative role;

—the role of the Court of Appeal in considering new evidence on appeal, including directing the investigation of allegations; and

—the arrangements for investigating alleged miscarriages of justice when appeal rights have been exhausted.

Addresses

Government Departments

Home Office, 50 Queen Anne's Gate, London SW1H 9AT.

Department of Health, Richmond House, 79 Whitehall, London SW1A 2NS.

Law Officers' Department, Attorney General's Chambers, Royal Courts of Justice, Strand, London WC2A 2LL.

Lord Advocate's Department, Fielden House, 10 Great College Street, London SW1P 3SL.

Lord Chancellor's Department, Trevelyan House, 30 Great Peter Street, London SW1P 2BY.

Northern Ireland Information Service, Stormont Castle, Belfast BT4 3ST.

Scottish Education Department (Social Work Services Group), 43 Jeffrey Street, Edinburgh EH1 1DN.

Scottish Home and Health Department, St Andrew's House, Edinburgh EH1 3DE.

Scottish Office, New St Andrew's House, Edinburgh EH1 3SX.

Other Organisations

Criminal Injuries Compensation Board, Whittington House, 19 Alfred Place, London WC1E 7EJ.

Howard League for Penal Reform, 322 Kennington Park Road, London SE11 4PP.

Legal Aid Board, Newspaper House, Great New Street, London
EC4A 3BN.

Liberty, 21 Tabard Street, London SE1 4LA.

National Association for the Care and Resettlement of Offenders,
169 Clapham Road, London SW9 0PU.

National Association of Prison Visitors, 46b Hartington Street,
Bedford MK41 7RN.

Royal Commission on Criminal Justice, Whittington House, 19
Alfred Place, London WC1E 7LU.

Scottish Association for the Care and Resettlement of Offenders,
53 George Street, Edinburgh EH2 2ET.

Scottish Legal Aid Board, 44 Drumsheugh Gardens, Edinburgh
EH3 7SW.

Further Reading

Annual Reports and Statistics

Commissioner of Police of the Metropolis	HMSO
Criminal Statistics (England and Wales)	HMSO
Criminal Statistics (Scotland)	HMSO
Crown Prosecution Service	HMSO
Her Majesty's Chief Inspector of Constabulary	HMSO
Judicial Statistics	HMSO
Police Complaints Authority	HMSO
Her Majesty's Chief Inspector of Prisons	HMSO
Northern Ireland Prison Service	HMSO
Prison Service (England and Wales)	HMSO
Prisons in Scotland	HMSO
Serious Fraud Office	HMSO

Other Official Publications

			£
The 1988 British Crime Survey. Home Office Research and Planning Unit Paper No 111. ISBN 0 11 340965 6.	HMSO	1989	10.00
Crime, Justice and Protecting the Public. Home Office, Cm 965. ISBN 0 10 109652 6.	HMSO	1990	6.20

£

*Custody, Care and Justice: the Way Ahead for
the Prison Service in England and Wales.*
Home Office, Cm 1647. ISBN 0 10 116472 6.   HMSO   1991   11.20

*A Digest of Information on the Criminal Justice
System.* Home Office Research and Statistics
Department.   Home Office   1991

Organising Supervision and Punishment in the Community.
Available free from the Home Office (C6 Division).

*Prison Education. The Government Reply to
the Second Report from Education, Science and
Arts Committee, Session 1990–91.*
Cm 1683. ISBN 0 10 116832 2.   HMSO   1991   3.25

*Royal Commission on Criminal Justice: Home
Office Memoranda.* ISBN 0 86252 809 7.   Home Office   1991   9.00

*The Sentence of the Court: A Handbook for
Courts on the Treatment of Offenders.*
ISBN 0 11 340985 0.   HMSO   1990   4.25

Tackling Crime in the United Kingdom.   Home Office   1990

Written by Reference Services,
Central Office of Information.

Printed in the UK for HMSO.
Dd294981   c30   8/92